I0438340

TAKING BACK AMERICA

TAKING BACK AMERICA

Robert R. Rider

Copyright © 2009 by Robert R. Rider.

Library of Congress Control Number: 2009907460
ISBN: Softcover   978-1-4415-5604-2

All rights reserved. No part of this book may be reproduced or transmitted in any form
or by any means, electronic or mechanical, including photocopying, recording, or by
any information storage and retrieval system, without permission in writing from the
copyright owner.

This book was printed in the United States of America.

To order additional copies of this book, contact:
Xlibris Corporation
1-888-795-4274
www.Xlibris.com
Orders@Xlibris.com
66344

CONTENTS

One:	On the Federal, State and Local Level, Clean Out the Den of Thieves	14
Two:	Make New Rules Regulating Government Officials Perks	16
Three:	Replace the Tax Code	18
Four:	Tackle the Foreign Aid Problem	20
Five:	Solve the Illegal Emigration Problem	22
Six:	Review All Trade Agreements	24
Seven:	Stop Jail Overcrowding and Restore Order of Law	25
Eight:	Work On the Drug Problem	27
Nine:	Restore Freedom of Religion	28
Ten:	Pass A Bill On "Truth in Campaigning"	30
Eleven:	Solve the Lobbyist Situation	31
Twelve:	Look Into the Union Situation	32
Thirteen:	Restore Patriotism Across the Country	34
Fourteen:	Truth in Advertising	35
Fifteen:	Restoring Our Individual Rights	36
Sixteen:	Making Laws From the Bench	38
Seventeen:	Stop Frivolous Lawsuits	39
Eighteen:	Find A Way To Overcome the ACLU	41
Nineteen:	Do Away With Political Correctness	42
Twenty:	Solve the Marriage Problem	43
Twenty One:	The Military Situation	44
Twenty Two:	Review the United Nations Charter	46
Twenty Three:	Solve the Oil and Gas Problem	48
Twenty Four:	Look Into Non-Profit Organizations	50
Twenty Five:	Cost Consuming Programs, Federal, State, Local Levels	51
Twenty Six:	Solve the Social Security Problems	52
Twenty Seven:	Reducing the National Debt	54

Twenty Eight: The English Language 55
Twenty Nine: Government Aid 56
Thirty: Abortion 58
Thirty One: Parental Rights 60
Thirty Two: Movies and Television 61
Thirty Three: Biased News Networks 63
Thirty Four: The Us Postal Service and
                the Us Forest Service 64
Thirty Five: Change the Rules On
                Leftover Campaign Contributions.............................65

Handout Information 69

TAKING BACK AMERICA

The reasons for me writing this book are two-fold and they must each take place before the other can happen. First of all I want to restore this nation to be the godly nation that our fore-fathers set it up to be in the very beginning. Following are a few things I would like the people to know to help them understand that this was once a godly nation.

In the:

Library of Congress—The Ten Commandments
U.S. Supreme Court—Moses
Ronald Regan Building—The Ten Commandments
National Archives—The Ten Commandments
The White House—John Quincy Adam's prayer
The Library of Congress—"Ignorance is a curse of God"
The District Court—Scriptures
The Washington Monument—"Praise be to God"
Chapel in the U.S. Capitol—George Washington praying
Lincoln's Second Inaugural Address—The word "God" throughout
U.S. Currency—"In God We Trust"

I am sure there are many more places where you can find God in our national background. I am so saddened by what has happened to this country. I believe that the ACLU is the culprit but the government has allowed it to happen. They have allowed the word "God" to be taken out of our schools, where it cannot be spoken out loud. How sad this is and it just breaks my heart. This will be covered in chapter nine.

The second reason for this book is to restore this nation back to the design and purpose our forefathers meant it to be. My question is this, "Does the government of today even come close to resembling the government designed by our forefathers?" I think they would surely turn over in their graves if they could see this government we have today. I heard a talk show host say "Forget the Declaration of Independence, the people should just do what is right." I think he was wrong on both points of his statement. We must keep the Declaration of Independence on our minds at all times for it tells us what to do with a government like we have today. As we strive to take back our country, let us examine some of the things I have taken from this very important document.

"We hold these truths to be self evident. That all men are *created equal*, that they are *endowed by their creator* with certain *unalienable rights*, that among these are *Life, Liberty*, and the *Pursuit of Happiness*." Do the people running this country think we are equal to them? I think not. We do have life for what it's worth. What liberty we do have is slowly being taken away. Are we happy? From what I have been seeing and hearing a lot of people are not happy.

The Declaration continues, "Governments are instituted among men during their just powers from *the consent of the governed*. It goes on "Whenever any form of government becomes destructive of these ends *it is the right of the people to alter or abolish it and to institute new government.*" And further on, "But when a long train of abuses and usurpations pursuing invariably the same object evidences a design to reduce them under absolute despotism (tyrant), *It is their right, it is their duty* to throw off such government and to provide new guards for their future security*." This is something we must do!

On the commentator's other point, "The people just have to do what is right." The problem with that statement is that today a lot of people don't know what is right. How could they possibly know when, from the cradle to the grave, they are constantly being blasted by movies, TV and News Networks containing all the bad things that are corrupting this country? A sitting president can have sex with a young girl in the White House and lie to the Grand Jury and not be punished. People throughout the government get caught in all kinds of crimes and are never punished. If money is involved they just pay it back when they get caught. This attitude has been accepted by the general public, so now it is, "Do what you can get away with until you get caught."

I heard another commentator say, "Never has a government been overthrown from the ballot box, but only through armed rebellion." I say, "Those same people who could be strong enough to overthrow the sitting government by use of arms could be strong enough to overthrow the sitting government through the ballot box." It would take the same amount of people either way and would have far less bloodshed.

So how do the people take back a government that is completely out of control and is not anything like our forefathers meant the government to be? I realize the great enormity of the task that this book covers. The very fact that it can happen if enough people would just believe. Most things in this book have been written just as if we had already taken back the country.

We have to create a new party. The two party system has failed us. I know other parties have been formed and have not become successful, but I think that the climate is now right for a new party and hopefully, some of the people from those parties that have failed, will join us. We need a name for this new party. I feel that the name should relate to what we are trying to do, *Taking Back America*, After much thought I have come up with the name "*The People's Party of America.*" I think after the very first person has signed up we will have become a party *of* the people, *for* the people and *by* the people. We will strive to do what is best for the country and the people. We will also make safeguards so that it's the people controlling the government and not the government controlling the people. We have to realize that this country is what it is today because the people have gone along with believing the politicians' lies election after election. I think by allowing this, it has gotten to the point that the politicians' think we are all just a bunch of dummies that will believe anything and will vote accordingly. Every election we get lies and promises, lies and promises and after the winners get in we find out that they could care less about the people and do just as they please. They are there to seek fame, power and to pad their own pockets, yes greed. The people in power do not care one bit about this great nation, or at least, they don't act like it. Sorry folks, but those are the facts.

The first thing we must do is find enough people who are sick and tired of what the government is doing to the people and the nation. Those people who say "I am sick and tired of it all but I am just one person, what can I do?" (I will repeat this later) We must get the people of this nation to realize just how much power the people have as a group. We must have those very same people register with our party until we have enough members to have the party recognized. And we must strive to become a party in every state in the union. This can be done in the beginning from home computers with printers to make printouts to be handed out on the street by volunteers. The handouts should explain our party, what it stands for and what it's goals are. I believe that this is the right time to get out our voice to the public, that public who are very tired of old politics. There are tax revolts and talk of seceding from the Union. Just maybe, enough people are fed up and have been looking for a way to do something about it. All of these people would sign up and contribute to *The People's Party* and quit giving to other parties or to people from other parties. A trust fund would have to be set up in every state in the Union. Hopefully, someone would step forward in each state to handle these funds and would be accountable to keep track of every dollar and to see that these funds would be deposited into the trust fund for The People's Party. These people would be considered party officials and would later become eligible for party positions in elections held later on. Believe me, there would be many party positions available after *The People's Party* wins a general election. There would be people from our party replacing the President, most members of Congress, Governors, Mayors and many other positions that the voters decide on. You might say, "What is going to keep these people accountable and trustworthy to handle these funds?" I believe any person trying to start up a new party in whatever state will have the heart required by *The People's Party* and with that heart he, or she, will have to be trusted.

Later on, before a person can hold any office or officiate in any party position on the federal, state, or local level, they must sign an agreement that they will not seek fame, fortune or power while seeking or holding office in *The People's Party*. The signed agreement can be used for removal of that person from any office held. Hopefully, by this time, someone will have stepped forward to lead this party. Then all signed agreements would be handed over to him or her. I have set up an email address (*bobfree@sbcglobal.net*) and will be available to help anyone until someone steps forward to lead the party. This signed agreement must be done to insure that this party will keep the people and nation first and foremost in their minds and that this nation does not return to the old politics. There is no way someone from our party seeking a political office can not obtain some fame, some power and a good income, but they did not seek those things and with *The People's Party* attitude, will not consider these thing important to themselves.

After we have been officially recognized as a party and compete in a general election, we must win by a mandate in almost every state in the union. I can hear it now, "What has this man been smoking? What a dreamer. Is he crazy?" Well, I can assure you, brothers and sisters, I do not smoke at all, I don't think I am a dreamer and until now, I have not been considered crazy. I do have a dream however, and that is to see this country returned to the country it once was. One full of integrity, full of pride, full of the rule of law, full of patriotism, full of *God*, full of national purpose and not government purpose. I love this country and pray we get it back.

The people of this country must come to realize just how much power they have. I know I have said this before but it is well worth repeating. Hopefully, this book and the call to the people to rise up at the ballot box will make it possible to take control of this country once again. If that happens the victory will be ours. I have great confidence this can happen and must happen. Otherwise the rest of this book is mute. But it may keep people thinking on just what can happen if the people pull together. Following is a list of things that could happen when we take back this country. I want *The People's Party of America* to know that this list is my suggestions and subject to change if *The People's Party* so chooses. They would be in power but they must remember not to do anything against the constitution or anything that would return them to the old politics as usual. Some of the chapters may seem very harsh and cruel but keep in mind, I was thinking of what was best for the nation and people. (The list is not arranged in order of importance).

On the federal, state and local level, clean out the den of thieves. (See chapter one)

Make new rules and laws regulating government officials perks. (See chapter two)

Replace the tax code. (See chapter three)

Tackle the foreign aid problem. (See chapter four)

Solve the illegal immigration problem. (See chapter five)

Review all trade agreements. (See chapter six)

Solve the jail overcrowding problem and restore the rule of law. (See chapter seven)

Work on the drug problem. (See chapter eight)

Restore freedom of religion to this country. (See chapter nine)

Pass a bill on "Truth in campaigning." (See chapter ten)

Solve the lobbyist situation. (See chapter eleven)

Look into the union situation. (See chapter twelve)

Restore patriotism to this country and, most definitely in our schools. (See chapter thirteen)

Pass a bill on "Truth in Advertising." (See chapter fourteen)

Pass new legislation to cover "Individual rights." (See chapter fifteen)

Pass legislation making it illegal to make law from the bench. (See chapter sixteen)

Stop or limit frivolous lawsuits. (See chapter seventeen)

Find a way to stop and overcome the ACLU. (See chapter eighteen)

Dissolve "Political Correctness". (See chapter nineteen)

Solve the marriage situation. (See chapter twenty)

Review the military situation. (See chapter twenty one)

Review the United Nations charter. (See chapter twenty two)

Solve the oil and gas problem. (See chapter twenty three)

Look into Non-Profit Organizations. (See chapter twenty four)

Look into all cost consuming problems on the Federal, State and Local level. (See chapter twenty five)

Solve the Social Security problem. (See chapter twenty six)

Reduce the national debt. (See chapter twenty seven)

Solve the "English Language" problem. (See chapter twenty eight)

Look into all Government Aid Programs. (See chapter twenty nine)

Look into the abortion problem. (See chapter thirty)

Restore "Parental Rights". (See chapter thirty one)

Clamping down on movies and television. (See chapter thirty two)

Finding ways to stop biased News networks. (See chapter thirty three)

Look into the US Postal Service and US Forest Service. (See chapter thirty four)

Change the rules on leftover Campaign Contributions. (See chapter thirty five)

CHAPTER ONE

ON THE FEDERAL, STATE AND LOCAL LEVEL, CLEAN OUT THE DEN OF THIEVES

When I speak of "den of thieves," I am talking about all those people holding office that have brought changes upon the people for many years now. It has been a slow progressive change that has eroded the government into that which we have today.

I am putting this chapter first because it is the most important and has to be done before any of the other chapters can be successfully brought about. Of course, when writing this I assume that, *We the people* have won in a General Election. Let us say, whether you are a Republican or Democrat, and have strong convictions on your party's policies and you have just won the election in a presidential race, well, all of that is easy to understand. But now that your party is in office, the very same people that lied to you to get into office and spent millions of your dollars to get into office are now, the truth be known, were only seeking fame, fortune and power. They have won and now they could care less about you or the country. They may make policies that look good to you but, believe me, they are designed to help themselves rule over the people. There has to be a time *when people will say, "Enough is enough".*

One of the first things we can do is vote out all incumbents in the upcoming congressional races. After as many incumbents as possible have been voted out then *The People's Party,* having won the national election, could submit a test bill to the House and Senate that would require all members of Congress to start contributing to the Social Security System and give up their current government retirement. Those who vote against the bill would be targeted in their own states for recall or impeachment, whichever is within the law in their individual states. This would continue until all those holding office have been removed. This can be done because, *"We, the people"*, have received a mandate in all states and now have control of the government in all states. Those U.S. Congressmen would be replaced by electing people from every state to *The People's Party*. I can hear it now, "But none of them have any experience, how can they run the country?" My answer to that is this, "All those experienced men that we now have in office, this country would be better off if they would just stay home and collect their paychecks." Their experience is to know how to cheat, lie, money grab and hold themselves in high esteem. Most of what they do is bad for the country and people anyway. They all have to be voted out, one bad apple can spoil the whole barrel. I am sure there are some good and honest men who are voted into the U.S. Congress. They may stay honest and good for about two weeks. They get bullied, they get bad office space, they are not allowed to serve on important committees until they become team players. What chance do they have? Not only that, they will be slandered, scoffed at and lied about by the *liberal, biased press* if they do not go along and they speak out against what is going on. I speak about the Democrats here, of course. They are blanketed by the *liberal, biased press.*

After all the sitting politicians have been replaced, then all the bills that have been submitted, by the president or congress, will be passed and signed into law by the President. This will start the clean-up of this country. While we have been taking control of the Federal Government, the same thing will have been going on at the state and local levels of government. I don't know what has been going on in other states, but the California State Government is a total mess. This state government, which is also controlled by the Democrats, have spent billions more than they have taken in. There is no rule of law, it's a joke. (see chapter 7) *We the people* must also control the state and local governments. Then we will be able to change or remove all the bad laws and make laws that are good for the people and country.

CHAPTER TWO

MAKE NEW RULES REGULATING GOVERNMENT OFFICIALS PERKS

We can save much money here. This has to be done after you have cleaned out the sitting politicians. The first thing to do would be for someone to submit a bill putting all members of the House and Senate into the Social Security System like everyone else. What's good for us should be good for them. Not only that, then they might not be so willing to rob it.

Then, the new House and Senate would pass a bill taking away all perks for all members of congress. No free food, no free gas, no free cars, no free drinks. All perks would be taken away. Some housing allowance could be allowed because they have to keep up two households. There would be no cuts in salaries but there would be many changes in their retirement plan. Some might say, "Why would anyone want to serve as a congressman?", and I say, "Exactly." Those new members of the House and Senate would be from *The People's Party of America*, and would only be wanting to do what is right for the people and the country. They would want to save the people's money instead of spending the people's money.

The new president would be getting all the perks and respect that any president has had in the past but, hopefully he would try to cut back whenever possible, to save money.

There should never be such a thing as diplomatic immunity for anyone. If you break the law, you pay the price. (See chapter 7)

The People's Party must strive to let the people know that just because you are a congressman does not mean you should be called "honorable". (That has to be earned) *The People's Party* winners must strive not to think they are great because they have been elected congressman. That does not make a person great but, a person's actions can make the position of congressman great.

CHAPTER THREE

REPLACE THE TAX CODE

While starting to write this chapter, I am wishing that I was a master mathematician, and a computer expert all rolled into one. I was able to find out the tax brackets that now exist. Ten percent being the lowest and thirty five percent being the highest, and many in between. You also have a lot of other taxes added on and many loopholes depending on who you are. Somewhere, I found out that the U.S. Government income was somewhere around two thousand six hundred fifty billion dollars. That's not enough, they want more. I will leave it to others to figure out the new tax brackets to be used under the new flat tax that I suggest we use. It will all have to be figured out after we have found out how much we have saved under all the new programs I have suggested. We also will have to figure out what we have saved just by staying within our balanced budget, which has not been done in years.

I propose a flat tax with the following scales:

Zero—five hundred dollars—No tax
Five hundred—one thousand—1%
One thousand—ten thousand—3%
Ten thousand—fifty thousand—5%
Fifty thousand—two hundred thousand—10%
Two hundred thousand—five hundred thousand—15%
Five hundred thousand and above—20%

There would be no tax deductions and taxes would still be withheld from wages. We would still need the I.R.S. to monitor the self employed and large corporations. We would be getting quite a savings on just getting rid of one hundred million miles of paper work. There would also be no refunds. I realize that this would be a blow to the tax preparers, but sometimes you just have to do what is right for the country and the people.

I tried to figure out something where everyone would be paying something except the very poor. Also, some people may still be getting some kind of government aid. That will be reviewed in Chapter 29.

While we are on the subject of taxes, we should submit a bill overturning the Death Tax. It should been done a long time ago. It is a very unfair tax and should be abolished.

CHAPTER FOUR

TACKLE THE FOREIGN AID PROBLEM

This, once again, is a problem that requires a statistician, computer whiz and someone with a lot of patience. I take the simple approach after coming up with some figures on foreign aid to be somewhere between 20.625 billion and 27.60 billion. I did find out that the following countries receive foreign aid from the United States and the quoted figures are from the year 2004.

Iraq—18.44 billion dollars
Israel—2.62 billion dollars
Egypt—1.87 billion dollars
Afghanistan—1.77 billion dollars
Columbia—0.57 billion dollars
Jordan—0.56 billion dollars
Pakistan—0.39 billion dollars
Liberia—0.21 billion dollars
Peru—0.17 billion dollars
Ethiopia—0.16 billion dollars
Bolivia—0.15 billion dollars
Turkey—0.15 billion dollars
Uganda—0.14 billion dollars
Sudan—0.14 billion dollars
Indonesia—0.13 billion dollars
Kenya—0.13 billion dollars

Total 27.60 billion dollars

The simple approach to me would be to stop foreign aid to all countries except those where the loss would have a direct effect on our national security. Most other countries could receive foreign aid for humanitarian supplies and food only, which should be monitored closely to ensure that the aid did not fall into the wrong hands. How much could be saved? Some billions of dollars. I also know that many countries receiving foreign aid do not like us and many support terrorism. We should stop or cut way back on foreign aid to Iraq. They should be spending some of those billions of dollars they are receiving from oil revenues. I know we may have agreements with some countries, but are those agreements in the best interest of this country? *The People's Party* would have to review everything because this country has not done anything right in a very long time.

CHAPTER FIVE

SOLVE THE ILLEGAL EMIGRATION PROBLEM

The simplest and the most sure way to solve this problem is to remember the rule of law. Illegal is illegal and when we, the American people get caught breaking the law, we are punished by fines, jail time or both. This may sound cold to some people but, I believe the answer would be to pass legislation that would take away everything that is attracting them here. No health care, no food stamps, no welfare, no benefits of any kind. Take very strict action on those who employ them, and prosecute, if necessary

The People's Party would pass legislation to build Employment Offices at each major point of entry into the U.S. Any company, agricultural or otherwise, would submit names of all they wish to hire temporarily, to the Border Employment Offices. Those being temporarily hired would be photographed, put into a national data base and given an I.D. card with their picture on it.

Those illegal people having been here five years or more, own homes and pay taxes would be required to become citizens within six months or they would be deported. We would set up citizenship classes to help them become citizens. Only those holding citizenship papers would be allowed to stay and work. The temporary documented workers from the Border Employment Office would also pay taxes according to the new tax structure. Employers having such job openings such as dishwashers, janitors, fast food workers, landscapers and any other low paying jobs must try to fill those positions from U.S. workers, such as students, the unemployed, the retired, people coming off welfare. If the jobs cannot be filled from the local population, then the people doing the hiring can submit names or worker requests to the Border Employment Offices.

All the people that have gone through the process and received a work card must be provided a clean work environment and ample wage to pay for food and lodging. Agricultural workers must be supplied with as clean as possible work environment, shelter, food, water and toilets. They must be paid an ample wage and the employer must withhold taxes according to the new flat tax.

Inspections would be held on a regular basis. I know some of this would cost us some money in the beginning but, we would be saving thousands of dollars by taking away the perks that the illegal aliens were getting. Anyone working here must be a citizen, hold work cards or green cards, which would also have to be documented and have the holder's pictures put on them.

I also realize that these programs must be installed at a time when most agricultural work has been completed and sometimes it may be necessary for the people doing the hiring to send workers to the Border Employment offices in small groups to get them legalized. All those details will have to be worked out.

CHAPTER SIX

REVIEW ALL TRADE AGREEMENTS

There have been many trade agreements that I am sure have not been in the best interests of the American workers and they should all be reviewed to determine if they may have or have not been in the best interest of the American People. I can think of one instance where the American people have been left out in the cold. I know that American companies move to other countries for cheap labor. I propose a bill that would allow those companies to stay in other countries but, they would have to pay the same wage there that they would be paying here. We would have to review NAFTA to see if the American people have come out on the negative end of the stick and, if so, do away with NAFTA. After looking into NAFTA, I found that there are many pros and cons on the subject. In most cases, NAFTA seems like a good program. An effort, however, must be made to make the balance of trade equal.

All trade agreements would have to be equal and not unbalanced. There must be a balance of trade. One thing for sure, we must stop truckers from other countries driving into the United States. We could not only save money here but put some American workers back to work.

I understand there have been very large trade deficits for the U.S. since day one. It must stop! It seems like the U.S. Government is trying to be Santa Claus to the rest of the world. There are places where *The People's Party* will be accused of being isolationist but, what we are doing is simply making trade equal and thinking of the U.S. citizens for a change.

CHAPTER SEVEN

STOP JAIL OVERCROWDING AND RESTORE ORDER OF LAW

I am sure, in the long run, we can save money here. This is one chapter that I am enjoying writing because the town that I live in is turning criminals loose daily. California, the state I now live in, the law is a joke. They could hand out enough speeding tickets to pay all the police, state and local pay checks and would be able to save lives at the same time. I propose *The People's Party* create a new Federal position, (Director over all penal code systems) who would be over all federal jails and prisons and have the duty to enforce the rule of law coming under federal authority.

We the people would ask Joe Arpeios or someone like him to head up this new government program. He could set up tent cities like the one in Arizona. We could acquire land in several desert states that could be acquired from the Bureau of Land Management. These tent cities would have to be in warm climates so the prisoners could be able to live in tents. We could pass laws in all states to allow use of these tent prisons to keep from jail overcrowding. This would relieve some local infrastructure from money problems and jail overcrowding which they now face.

The new *Director* would have full authority on running these tent cities. Rebellion would not be tolerated and anyone trying to escape or caught in the act of rioting could be shot. They would have no access to TV, radios or conjugal visits but, would have visitation according to the director and would have no touching of any kind. The director would have complete charge.

The Department of Justice started July 1, 1870 and had one Attorney General. Now we have ninety three U.S. Attorney Generals and three hundred fifty Assistant Attorneys. What a conglomerate of power. We would have to determine how many are really necessary. I doubt if anyone knows or cares how many are necessary, just more big government. At any rate, I would recommend one Attorney General for each state and reduce the number of assistants accordingly. After some research, I have found significant savings can be accomplished.

Of all the Departments of Law in the Department of Justice, I would recommend leaving them as is, except the Bureau of Prisons, the National Institute of Corrections, and the U.S. Marshall's office, which I would put under the *new Director over the U.S. Penal Code Systems.*

I think the overall budget of the Department of Justice is 43.5 billion. After all the waste that can be found here, I think we should look into all U.S. Government Programs. Not only would the tent cities stop the jail overcrowding, but would also strengthen the law in the penal code system. I feel it would also have an effect on the drug problem which is covered in Chapter 8. While we are on the subject of "rule of law", there are a couple of things that *The People's party* should clear up. We have to get the people's mind set away from feeling sorry for the bad guys and start looking out for the victims of crime. The police are really getting a bad deal. We should support the police and back them up all the way. Sure, there are some bad apples, but those bad cops should be taken care of and prosecuted accordingly by those departments designed to do so. Under no circumstance should any police officer be judged and condemned by the public. We should stand by the police at all costs.

Another thing that *The People's Party* should do is change the mind set of the people about natural disasters. They are not the fault of the government but the government, should try to give all the aid possible to the victims of natural disasters but should not be blamed above what they can do.

CHAPTER EIGHT

WORK ON THE DRUG PROBLEM

I only have a few suggestions on the drug problem. For one thing, we must put some teeth into the law. *The People's Party* must make laws such as the following:

Anyone doing drugs around children or selling any drugs to children and found guilty should be given mandatory prison time of twenty five years on the first offence and fifty to life for the second offence. Any adult found guilty of using drugs should get a mandatory sentence of five years and an additional sentence of five years for each time convicted of doing drugs after that. Anyone convicted of selling drugs to an adult would get a mandatory sentence of ten years in one of the tent cities. Anyone spending ten years in a tent city would not want to go back, I don't think, although there are always a few who are slow learners.

Also, (see chapter 5) if anyone has a drug problem and requests treatment, they should be given treatment and any other help they require. This must be done before any drug crime has been committed. If anyone on a drug treatment program commits a drug crime they will receive a mandatory sentence like anyone else.

We should lean over backwards helping the drug enforcement agents on any border. The fence at the border of Mexico should be completed right away and the drug enforcing agents be given all the tools they require to do their job, including electronic surveillance and aircraft.

CHAPTER NINE

RESTORE FREEDOM OF RELIGION

The People's Party must restore freedom of religion to this once godly country. A very wise man once said "Take God out of the country and you will have an immoral country." Well folks, just look around, that's exactly what we have.

The word "God" has been taken from our schools, school children are not allowed to pray, reference to God and Jesus not allowed in school Christmas programs, in fact, not even allowed to be called Christmas programs. Boundaries have been set on Christians throughout the country while other religions are ok. I just love what some children did when told that they could not refer to God or any part of religion in their graduation ceremony. A student giving a speech made a loud sneeze and in unison the whole class stood up and said "God bless you." Take that ACLU!

The way I understand it, the whole purpose of the separation of church and state was because our founding fathers did not want any church or religion to appear to be sponsored by the government which was the case in England. As *The People's Party*, we would have to make a law stating that it would be against the law for any one person or organization to threaten schools with law suits if they did not comply with their interpretation of the "separation of church and state." We would have to make a law overturning other laws against "freedom of religion"!

The People's Party would make a stand and say that each religion has it's own god and no religion shall be persecuted in these United States, make new coins with "in God we trust" visible for all to see and not on the edge where it is hardly visible, like the new dollar. We should all refuse to use the new dollar and turn it in for paper money. Maybe they will quit making it. I wish we could return to the old coinage that made our country proud, but it would be impossible with the price of metals today.

I just heard a song sent by email, but most people will not hear it because it is not politically correct. The song by the country band, Diamond Rio, goes like this. "In America, it's in God we trust". May we in America never stop putting our trust in God.

Schools must be able to say the Pledge of Allegiance in it's original form. School children must be able to pray at appropriate times. They must be able to have bible studies on school grounds and also at appropriate times. Also the U.S. Prosecuting Attorney would defend all schools being threatened by lawsuits concerning the separation of church and state.

The People's Party should make a law stating that no person or group shall persecute any church or religion and will be prosecuted if caught doing so.

CHAPTER TEN

PASS A BILL ON "TRUTH IN CAMPAIGNING"

We, *The People's Party*, should, without a doubt, pass a bill against making false statements, lies, distortions or accusations against any party or person or any ideas that a party or person has when they are running for office. They can be sued and may face criminal charges and prosecuted to the fullest extent of the law which, in this case, if found guilty would face jail time. These things are constantly being done on radio, TV, newspapers, rallies and debates. When false accusations can be proven, without a doubt, all those making the accusations will be prosecuted.

There has been so much lying going on, the voters are at a loss as to what they should believe and that, of course, is the purpose of the lies. Wouldn't it be wonderful if the voters could know the facts and vote according to their convictions? Today, the *liberal, biased Press* is much to blame because they support every thing the lying politicians say.

CHAPTER ELEVEN

SOLVE THE LOBBYIST SITUATION

I strongly recommend *The People's Party* do the following. Make it against the law to lobby anywhere in any congressional building or any US building or lobby with any congressman at any time or place.

We would set up a committee that would do nothing but receive lobbyist requests and allow only those requests that were a benefit to the country and people be submitted to the House and Senate for passage or rejection. This committee could be called the Congressional Lobbyist Committee and would be appointed by the new congress of *The People's Party*. This could save the people quite a sum of money because there are too many campaign promises being paid off to these lobbyists. Lobbyist requests are put into bills or passed as a part of another bill which is hidden so the people never know what has been passed into law.

CHAPTER TWELVE

LOOK INTO THE UNION SITUATION

The People's Party should find a way to make it fair for all workers, whether they are union workers or not. Put some teeth into the "Right to work" law or re-write it so that all workers are protected. Also, the law should state "Union dues cannot be used for political purposes" without a signed document from each union member. Also, the union member should be able to designate which party, or person, they want their dues to go to. As it is now, the unions get all the dues and gives to the Party or person they wish to support and that party or person will give a kick back to the unions. It happens all the time.

I believe the unions are a necessary evil. The union, in a lot of cases, is the only protection a worker has against company abuses and, in many companies, there are a lot of abuses. Sometimes the union accepts and files grievances against a company that have no merit. This is an unnecessary burden on the company. We should also look into the Teacher's Union, the Policemen's Union and the Firemen's Union. They put a lot of financial burden on cities and communities all across the nation. Even as I write this, there are some unions who would rather see a company go under than make the concessions necessary to help keep it afloat. I believe *The People's Party* should pass laws whether it be Federal, State, or Local that there should be no unionizing of government employees. Those that are government paid employees should get annual cost of living raises based on the cost of living.

Unions would not be able to force cities, towns, states or the US Government into bankruptcy. It's a vicious circle. The unions get everyone a five or ten percent raise, then the cost of living goes up accordingly, so no one wins.

This plan of action would get rid of teacher's unions, policemen's unions and firemen's unions which are all essential professions in every community. If the government employers, federal, state or local does not pay adequate, cost of living raises, the workers should have the right to file a complaint which would be settled by arbitration.

CHAPTER THIRTEEN

RESTORE PATRIOTISM
ACROSS THE COUNTRY

I know you cannot legislate laws telling people what to think or how to act. *The People's Party* should see to it that the following are protected:

The Pledge of Allegiance (including "under God")
The National Anthem
America The Beautiful
God Bless America
My Country Tis of Thee
Battle Hymn of the Republic

These songs should not only be allowed but encouraged in our schools and public gatherings. The government should not only back but also encourage making patriotic movies. We need to try and turn this country around and start building this country up instead of tearing it down. Anyone running this country down should be ridiculed by the President and the Congress, who are now of one mind. We need to find a way to stop people from thinking "me, me, me" and "mine". Some people today think "I am alive so I should have something coming to me." How do we stop that?

We should always honor our military who fight to keep us free. That subject will be covered in Chapter 21.

CHAPTER FOURTEEN

TRUTH IN ADVERTISING

After giving this topic much thought, I have come to the conclusion that making laws to require truth in advertising would be a very nice and wonderful thing, but overall, it would be bad for the national economy which would be bad for the people. We could, however, try to encourage truth in advertising and prosecute those advertisements that are blatantly outright lies and without facts. Do you realize all those ads out there that can cure everything in the book? If we bought all those items we could live forever. There are some truth in advertising laws out there that cover big ticket items like appliances, cars, houses, boats and real estate. Oh, and also electronic items. Also, I think there are laws protecting the public from bad contractors. We do need laws or enforce laws protecting the people against "here today and gone tomorrow" companies. They should be found and prosecuted. Also, there is the deep problem of sales on the internet that should be looked into.

Although it has nothing to do with truth, we should stop advertisements on all sexual oriented items, these are inappropriate for children's viewing. These advertisements could only be run after 12 a.m.

CHAPTER FIFTEEN

RESTORING OUR INDIVIDUAL RIGHTS

The People's Party should pass a new bill restoring our individual rights. Throughout the years many of our rights have been taken away. One of the most common is to own and keep property. In the past "Imminent Domain" meant that government could pay you what your property was worth and use the property for thoroughfares such as streets, highways, freeways and also building dams.

The railroads have taken land that wasn't even needed for Railroad Right of ways and then made millions when reselling it.

The US Supreme Court now says they can use "imminent domain" to take your land to make room for housing developments or anything else that would bring in higher taxes. *We The People*, should make laws to protect people from "imminent domain" when it's not for thoroughfare usage.

We The People should also make laws protecting people from intrusion on their property by those who steal, maim or do bodily harm. The law now seems to protect the lawbreaker and not the individual owning the property. We should pass a law making it lawful to shoot anyone coming onto a person's property to commit a harmful crime, but make it clear that the property owner must prove that the person shot was there to commit bodily harm in the process of committing the crime

We The People must protect the property owner if they are brought to court by any persons who have been harmed while committing a crime. We must turn society around so that the victims of crime are protected and not the law breakers. The law now says you can only shoot a person or persons if they break into your house with the intent of doing bodily harm. Not only that, but they must be shot inside the house. There have been cases where the property owner did bodily harm to a thief and ended up being sued. In one case the thief ended up with the property the owner was trying to protect. (See chapter 17 on Frivolous Law Suits) I can't see much difference of a criminal coming onto your property to do bodily harm or coming into your house to do bodily harm.

CHAPTER SIXTEEN

MAKING LAWS FROM THE BENCH

The way I understand it, laws are made by the Lawmakers and Judges are to enforce the laws if they are constitutional. I tried to find out just how many laws have been made from the bench, but was unable to do so. As near as I can figure out, Congress has the authority to not only overturn laws made from the bench but could also impeach or replace judges that have made laws from the bench. I wonder why this has not been done? Could it be that the people in Congress are just as liberal as the judges that make laws from the bench?

The People's Party, who now control the Congress should overturn these laws made from the bench and get rid of the judges that made them.

CHAPTER SEVENTEEN

STOP FRIVOLOUS LAWSUITS

The People's Party must stop frivolous litigation. Such lawsuits are a waste of time, waste of money for the court system, defending lawyers time and the money of the people involved in the lawsuits. I think there are already laws against frivolous lawsuits but are almost never enforced.

In the US Tax Court there can be penalties of up to twenty five thousand dollars. Rule #2, which I really don't quite understand, also covers non-criminal cases, where fines can also be handed out. Following are some examples of frivolous court filings.

Motion:

> to Kiss my—. (expletive deleted)
> To Behoove an inquisition
> for Restoration of sanity
> for Deinstitutionalization
> for Publicity
> to Vacate jurisdiction
> to Psychoanalysis
> to Impeach Judge Alaimo
> to Renounce citizenship
> for Skin change operation
> for Catered food service

Another good example is when a Washington D.C. judge sued a dry cleaning business for fifty four million. The dry cleaners lost the judges pants, which he had brought in for a ten dollar and fifty cent alteration. The cleaners refused the judge's demand for a large refund. The pants cost one thousand dollars. The list goes on and on.

Those lawyers that bring these law suits before the court should be fired and in some cases, lose their licence to practice law.

The People's Party should make an all out effort to see that these law suits stop. Take the case where a woman sued a fast food restaurant for millions because she spilled hot coffee on herself. How much do you think the woman got and how much did the lawyer get? Part of the problem is the people sitting on the juries. They will find any way they can to take money from any business and give it to the little person and their lawyers. Once again, we need to turn around the mind set of the people to think on what is right and what is justice.

CHAPTER EIGHTEEN

FIND A WAY TO OVERCOME THE ACLU

The ACLU picked a name that would sound good and patriotic to the populous, but in truth, they are tearing down America. This is made possible by misinterpreting the Constitution and not being challenged by Congress and the liberal press, which is the main stream press.

When *The People's Party* controls both houses of Congress, we can make laws defending the constitution, use the Attorney General's office to fight the law suits brought on by the ACLU and use all of our power to stop the flow of money funding the ACLU.

Brothers and sisters, this organization is one of the worst threats to this fine country. It must be stopped. I have tried to find out how many cases have been won or lost by the ACLU, but either no one seems to care or they are afraid to put it on the internet. I did find out that many court cases won by the ACLU were in one of the lower courts and has not reached the higher courts.

Have you ever wondered why the ACLU picks on individual states or communities about the separation of church and state? Why don't they pick on the US Government? Could it be because they know the US Government has the funds and power to win in the court system?

CHAPTER NINETEEN

DO AWAY WITH
POLITICAL CORRECTNESS

To me, this is the easiest chapter to write. *The People's Party* just needs the votes in congress to simply say "No more political correctness." This has been pushed on us by worthless people in congress. We then replace political correctness with common sense. I guess congress not having any common sense needed guide lines on how to act and talk and made everyone else do the same. The average person does not need guide lines on how to talk and think and do what is right. We don't need politicians telling us how to act, think and talk. Enough said.

The People's Party could, should and would make a law banning or getting rid of political correctness.

CHAPTER TWENTY

SOLVE THE MARRIAGE PROBLEM

Once again the politicians and the liberal media are trying to push something down our throats. They would like us to believe that one third of the Nation, or maybe even half, are gay. When *The People's Party* gets into office, they will have had a mandate in all the states. They would be able to pass a Constitutional Amendment, ratified by all the states, that "marriage is between a man and a woman only." The politicians have been going around the will of the people on this problem which seems like a popular thing to do today. We must do this to settle the argument once and for all.

CHAPTER TWENTY ONE

THE MILITARY SITUATION

It's about time the military get the recognition they so justly deserve and *The People's Party* are just the ones that can do that. First of all, the fighting men and women need a decent wage for what they do and a considerable increase in pay while serving in a combat zone. These wages would have to be determined after all costly programs have been cut and the party, for the first time in ages, working with a balanced budget.

Whenever possible, the military should be given what funds are necessary to advance the technology of fighting equipment. If and when, the Congress and the President decide military action is required and necessary funds approved, it should be up to the President and the military on how the action should be carried out and not the Congress except in the case of atomic warfare.

We should never again have wars run by the Congress influenced by demonstrations in the street. Nor shall Congress withhold funds after they have approved military action. The President being Commander-in-Chief over the military would use the military advisors provided him.

Personnel of all branches of the military should and would receive a proper, warm welcome home which would be sponsored by *The People's Party*.

Any person of the military, having been wounded in a military conflict would receive proper treatment and livelihood for the rest of their lives, or until they are able to return to work. Any person returning to civilian life must have the opportunity to return to the job they last held before entering the military. Those returning and having never worked, should receive assistance finding a job and receive unemployment until they do. But, of course, any slackers who won't work and won't look for work would be denied unemployment after a six month time.

All people having served their time in the military should be given the opportunity to attend a four year college or a trade school under the new G.I. Bill set forth by *The People's Party*.

CHAPTER TWENTY TWO

REVIEW THE UNITED NATIONS CHARTER

Hang on to your hats, folks, this is a tough one, but I will get right to it. The United Nations, as it stands, is one of the most useless organizations possible. It has no teeth and very little direction. As near as I can find out, the current budget is about 4.19 billion dollars and the United States portion is almost 1 billion dollars. What I propose is to request that the United Nations charter be amended and insist on the following changes.

No diplomatic immunity.
Set up an accounting system with annual audits.
The President cannot have any control over money.
Do away with sanctions, they are not effective and a waste of time.
New resolutions should be acted upon immediately.
Do not allow warring members and those involved in terrorism to hold office or vote.
At no time can the UN level taxes on any country or nation.
At no time can the UN draft into the UN Service any person from any country.

I will admit that I do not know everything there is to know about the UN and some things, I suggest may be extreme, but the way I look at it, while we are cleaning up all the bad things that this government has made and accepted, why not go all the way and change the things that are not good for the people of this and other countries? I am a simple man and can only see what is in front of me. We must put some teeth into the UN.

If the UN rejects the US request for changes in the UN Charter, the US Government, under the control of *The People's Party* should stop all money going to the UN and withdraw from the UN.

By withdrawing from the UN we would be saving about one billion dollars a year. Hopefully, the UN would agree to the changes with the threat of losing US funds and withdrawal from the UN.

I realize there may be some things I suggest that may have an effect on national security, but if not, plow ahead. Probably much research will have to be done on this problem because it is so complex.

CHAPTER TWENTY THREE

SOLVE THE OIL AND GAS PROBLEM

After *The People's Party* has control of the presidency and congress, whoever holds the office of president should call a meeting with all US Oil Companies and tell them that the new administration would like to work with them to solve many problems that now exists to provide fuel and gas, at a reasonable cost for the American people. Tell them if they refuse to cooperate and work with the President, he would, with the help of Congress, threaten to nationalize all US oil operations. The President could offer them many incentives to work with him. He could offer them a good, reasonable profit, remove the national gas tax, open up oil drilling off the coasts and in many areas where they are not allowed to drill. An offer of oil from the National Reserves until they get new wells drilled and then they must pay the oil back.

In return, the Oil Companies must build two refineries each in the next five years. They must agree that they would no longer operate as a monopoly, (which they are) and each one operate independently. No more raising gas prices on the same day. All gasoline trucks must be marked and used by the oil company hauling and selling the gas. No exchanging of gas. All companies must work independently.

All oil companies would be monitored on a regular basis by an independent committee, set up for that purpose. There would be no exporting of any oil or oil products and all imported oil must be imported at a price equal to the price of crude taken from the wells in the US.

I believe the oil companies could make a good profit from selling gas at $2.00 a gallon. If not, the oil companies would have to show a price that is acceptable and would give them a good profit margin and still keep the pump prices at a minimum. No longer would windfall profits be allowed.

We must break the oil companies monopoly. As it is now, the oil companies seem to own our government. I believe that the US President, after such a meeting, would need double protection for his life but it wouldn't matter because, in the event of the president losing his life, someone just like him would come into power from *The People's Party* no one person or group would ever be able to change that. You can kill the man but not the idea or movement. I wish there was a better way to break the monopoly that the oil companies have today, but there isn't.

We must also look into alternative energy sources such as wind, solar and atomic power plants.

CHAPTER TWENTY FOUR

LOOK INTO NON-PROFIT ORGANIZATIONS

The People's Party should set new rules and guidelines governing non-profit organizations. Non-Profit organizations should be made to show that 90% of all donations go to the cause the organization was set up for. There are too many people making large profits and some getting rich on heading up non-profit organizations. These organizations should be monitored on a regular basis. This should be good for the people and all the good causes that are out there. I know it would be hard to keep track of all the donations taken in and, also, what was spent. Any organization not reporting all the donations and getting caught not putting 90% to the cause would be prosecuted and made to pay to the cause, all that was withheld over 10%.

CHAPTER TWENTY FIVE

COST CONSUMING PROGRAMS, FEDERAL, STATE, LOCAL LEVELS

I am sure there are many programs out there that are a benefit to elected officials only and not a benefit to the people. They have been added to bills that are essential to pay off someone that helped get the official elected. *We The People* must rescind or overturn these bills. I am sure we can save money here. It is time the elected officials start to think about the people that elected them and not themselves and their pals and buddies. *The People's Party* need to change laws and make new laws that are a benefit to the people.

I know that *The Den of Thieves* is just as bad in many states and cities across America and could be taken care of at the ballot box just as we did at the federal level. In my state alone, we could save millions of dollars by just repairing the roads, highways and freeways first and then go back and beautify them if funds are available.

Is California the only state where you see many men standing around leaning on a shovel or just talking? I think not. Many cost consuming programs will be covered in Chapter 29.

CHAPTER TWENTY SIX

SOLVE THE SOCIAL SECURITY PROBLEMS

We the People should make many changes to the Social Security System. Following are some suggestions that I think should be done:

Make a law saying the Federal Government cannot, for any reason, take money from the Social Security fund.

Make a law stating that only those people that have contributed to the fund can use the funds for retirement.

The only exception would be dependent children going through college, dependent children who have medical handicaps or people who have worked but are now unable to work because of medical or physical handicaps.

People coming to this country, old enough to retire but have not contributed, would not be eligible for benefits and benefits would stop for those already drawing benefits.

No one in prison could draw benefits and their time in prison would not count as work when they get out. Only the time worked before and after prison would count.

After *We The People* find out what money the general fund has after all the savings and the amount of income from the new tax code and living with a balanced budget, we should start paying back some of the money the den of thieves has taken from the Social Security Funds for many years. The Social Security Fund should start building up fast under these new rules and laws.

CHAPTER TWENTY SEVEN

REDUCING THE NATIONAL DEBT

After all the changes, *The People's Party* have made, we would not be increasing the national debt and, once again, depending on how much the General Fund grows and we have covered all expenditures, then we can start paying off the national debt. As I write this, the national debt has grown so high that we may never get it paid off. Still, that would be one of our goals. No one knows how far this administration will take us into debt.

We should also make a law that the US Government can not spend more than it takes in. Of course, as long as we are in power that will never happen. The people have to live by these rules and so should the government.

CHAPTER TWENTY EIGHT

THE ENGLISH LANGUAGE

Once again, *The People's Party*, should submit and pass a constitutional amendment making English the official language of the United States. When we go to other countries where they speak a language other than English, we are expected to learn their language. We should set up English speaking classes run by volunteers, if possible, or even government run, if need be. I have taught English as a second language (ESL) in my home and also at church. Churches and schools could be reimbursed by the government for space and for teachers' wages. They could also teach reading to help people become citizens.

We would also add this amendment, "that all documents and directions for anything will be printed in the English Language only."

CHAPTER TWENTY NINE

GOVERNMENT AID

We The People must look into all aspects of the Government Aid programs such as Medicare, Food stamps, Welfare and School Lunches. I am sure we can save much money here. Is Medicare good for the country and people? I don't know, but we should look into it and fix it if it's broken.

Now food stamps and welfare are another matter. All those people on welfare and capable of working, should be made to work. State and local governments should supply community jobs such as beautifying streets and parks, building trails, picking up litter along streets, highways and freeways and many other government projects. They should receive at least minimum wage and should pay taxes at the appropriate level under the new flat tax schedule. The US Government would have to reimburse the state and local governments for money spent on wages.

Food stamps would only be issued if wages were inadequate, depending on how many are in the family and to those with disabilities, that make them unable to work.

School lunches would only be given to those families making less than $10,000 a year. I am basing my figures on the way the economy is today. Everything would have to be re-evaluated after *The People's Party* has been in office a short time. The economy would change very fast because, not only would we be operating within our budget, but we would have eliminated many costly programs. Inflation would go down and the standard of living would go up very quickly.

We would do away with government grants, but would continue giving four year student loans which must be paid back within ten years after graduating or wages would be garnisheed.

Food stamps would be given to citizens only. For those people who have low income jobs, *We The People* would make trade schools and student loans available. The government would monitor all student loans and repayments very closely.

I am sure there are many other programs out there that we know nothing about, but we will check them out.

CHAPTER THIRTY

ABORTION

Once again, *The People's Party*, having received a mandate at the federal and state levels, would have the opportunity to, not only, save money but do what is right in God's eyes. The Supreme Court has already made a decision on abortion so, at the present time, we have to abide by their decision, but will seek ways to overturn it. We can, however, save money and limit abortions. We must see that the government does not spend one dime on abortions. The Hyde Amendment limits government funding for abortions to rape, incest and when a woman's life is in danger, none of which is the fault or responsibility of the government.

The present government has found ways to fund abortions, one of which is grants. The US Government sets aside 400 billion for grants that are interest free and never have to be repaid. Planned Parenthood receives 270 million a year in grants. Medicare also funds abortions if a woman's life is in danger. There is government funding for teaching abortion procedures. Seventeen states have funding for abortions but, we will also be in control of state governments, so we can change that.

I cannot understand the mind set that many people have, that it is OK to save the whales, seals, spotted owls, all of which is at the expense of someone's livelihood and, yet, think it is OK to take the life of a little baby. They say the animals have no one to care for and protect them. The little babies, also have no one to stand up and protect them until now. Worse yet is taking the life of a baby after it is almost completely out of the birth canal.

What has this country become? It has become a very sick country and it's mostly due to *Liberalism.*

CHAPTER THIRTY ONE

PARENTAL RIGHTS

Slowly but surely, our rights have been taken away by the government, one of which is parental rights. Anyone who has children has the responsibility of raising and taking care of their children. That includes teaching them right from wrong. Now we can only discipline them according to the government standards. How could this have ever happened? *Liberalism*, again. Parents should be able to spank their children, which is from the bible and has been the case in this country for many years. The government should only step in when excessive punishment is used resulting in bodily harm. (Bodily harm is not a red rear-end) After all the rules and laws, the government has put upon the people, there has been an increase in child abuse every year.

Children should not be able to sue their parents (more *Liberalism*). Until a girl is 18, the parents should have control over when she can take birth control pills. They, also, should be the first to know when a girl becomes pregnant and should be the one to help her decide what should happen to the baby, keep it or give it up for adoption.

The government should stay out of people's private lives and *The People's Party* would see that they did.

CHAPTER THIRTY TWO

MOVIES AND TELEVISION

I write this chapter as a moral issue. We know we can't censor the movies and television but we can and should pass laws that change the rating system. We would be in control of the FCC so we could make many changes. Changing the time when certain TV programs could be shown and revising the rating system for both TV and movies. The TV and movie makers have had plenty of time and opportunity to regulate themselves and every year they get worse. I would suggest the FCC make the following changes to the ratings.

G—Movies on TV and programming on TV that has no sex, no violence greater than the old westerns, where the good guys always win. No blood, no dirty language of any kind, no nudity. This rating could be shown at any time day or night.

PG—Movies on TV and programming on TV that would have no nudity, no passionate sex scenes, mild violence, not showing a lot of blood, mild language, not using four letter words. These movies and TV could be shown after 10 pm.

M—Movies on TV and programming on TV having mild sex scenes, mild language, not using four letter words, cartoon programs, like The Simpsons, that teach our children to disrespect parents, teachers, police officers and law enforcement, in general, no nudity, no violence, showing a lot of blood. This rating could only be shown on TV after 12 am.

R & X—These ratings are virtually the same showing nudity, sex scenes, very bad language. They must not show actual sex acts or penetration, have a lot violence showing a lot of blood. R and X movies and programming could be shown only after 2 am.

No movies or programs would be able to show disrespect for country, rule of law, ethnic groups, persons or churches of any kind. I realize, in a way, this may look like censoring, but it really isn't.

We can encourage law suits, fines and jail time for those that choose not to follow the FCC guideline set forth by *The People's Party*. All theater movies could be shown at any time but must carry the new ratings set forth by the FCC. R and X TV movies and programming is actually smut and should be banned, Period. Unfortunately, we can't do that and the producers know there is a large audience out there. It's really a shame because some of the R rated movies and programs really have a good story line.

CHAPTER THIRTY THREE

BIASED NEWS NETWORKS

Now we are faced with the issue of Freedom of the Press. We all know that journalism has been thrown out the window with the bath water. I wonder just what they teach now in a Journalism Class? I can just hear it now "The important thing to remember is this, just say what you want, do what you want and as long as we stick together and have the *Liberal, biased media* behind us we are OK."

The *Liberal, biased media* are not concerned with facts because they have no one to challenge them and they think no one cares. Well, Folks, there are a lot of people who care and *The People's Party* may not be able to censor what is written but we sure can make laws encouraging lawsuits and prosecution of all out lies and slander where news networks are not able to back up a story.

In the old days, newspapers and TV News Networks were always being careful not to be sued. Today, all the liberal News Networks don't care because the people in power are behind them regardless of what they say. Dare we leave them in power? I pray not.

CHAPTER THIRTY FOUR

THE US POSTAL SERVICE AND
THE US FOREST SERVICE

I think these two Government Programs are over extended and not cost efficient. The US Postal Service has been hit hard by the on-line E-mail and just keeps raising the cost of postal stamps. We might just be better off turning this program over to a private company with the same protections that the Postal Service now has.

We must get the US Forest Service out of the lumber business. The Forest Service was set up to manage the forests. Today they are trying to manage everything that lives in the forest. I know *The People's Party could save much money here.*

CHAPTER THIRTY FIVE

CHANGE THE RULES ON LEFTOVER CAMPAIGN CONTRIBUTIONS

When a person has run for the office of President, Congress, Governor, Mayor or any other elected official, win or lose, they must return all left over donations as follows,

The US President and US Congress to the US Treasury, the Governors to the State Treasury, the Mayors to the City Treasury.

If a person uses their own money, along with contributions, they can keep the contributions up to the amount of money they used from their own pocket and turn in the rest.

Too many politicians are receiving large nest eggs from left over contributions. The money donated was to help someone gain a position and not to be added to their bank roll.

In conclusion, there are a few things that I would like to refresh the people's memory on. Please read again that portion of the Declaration of Independence telling us what to do when a government gets out of control, and this government is, and has been out of control for a long time. I would like to let the people of *The People's Party* to know what to expect from all the people in power today. At first they will laugh and scoff, make jokes until the people start joining The Party and contributing to us. Then they will try to tear us and our beliefs apart. The ones that are going to be most upset by this book are the "Den of Thieves", at all levels of government, Gays, Tax Preparers, Foreign Aid Recipients, Illegal Aliens, Criminals, Drug Lords, the biased News Media, Lobbyists, Unions, Liberal Judges, Lawyers, ACLU, United Nations, Oil Companies, Abortionists, Hollywood and TV News Networks.

I realize that all those people carry a lot of votes, but I urge the people joining *The People's Party* not to be discouraged by this. Whatever you do, do not give up your principles to get votes from any of these people. That is what has slowly happened in the past and you can see where it has led us. Besides, many of those people are going to be discouraged and disenchanted and will continue to become more so in the future. Because this government is going to get worse and worse. In order for *The People's Party* to get off the ground, we need a list of things that we stand for so we can make up brochures as handouts on the streets of every state in the Union. Whoever is making up the handouts should also list a phone number and email address so people can contact them, when seeking information on what to do. The list could also be used to form a party platform later on.

I am not stupid and I realize all that I propose in this book is a mighty task and it is my hope that someone who is a great organizer would step forward early, take over and get it off the ground. It would be even better if an organizer and someone with money would get involved.

HANDOUT INFORMATION

We The People support:

All business, big and small.
Enforcing the rule of law.
Individual rights.
The Constitution.
Freedom of the press, when not biased.
Law Enforcement Officers and Firemen.
Putting God back into America.
Gay rights, but not in marriage.
Fair tax laws.
Balanced Foreign Trade.
Putting teeth into the United Nations Organization
Getting rid of the ACLU.
Stopping illegal immigration.
Balancing the Budget.
Eliminating Jail overcrowding.
Stopping Lobbyists.
Restoring patriotism.
A strong Military.
Our fighting men and women.
Low gas prices.
Strengthening our Social Security Trust Fund.
Parental rights.
Rights of unborn babies.
Home schooling and vouchers.
Freedom of religion

I am sure there are many more good causes we will be supporting. Some will be discovered later, after we have cleaned out the bad things.

To all of those people that are going to be "mad enough to kill", I say this to you, "You can kill a person, but you will never kill an idea or movement". A good idea will spread like wildfire and this is a good idea of taking back this country. This book just might be the catalyst needed to turn this country around. The people are so frustrated, feeling helpless and thinking there is nothing they can do. They think "I am just one person and I have no power," but you do.

They hold Tax Revolts, Tea Parties and some even threaten to secede from the Union. What do they get? Ridiculed and called "Fox News Extremists" by *The Liberal, Biased press*. I hope, I pray that this book will show them what to do and how to do it.

The biggest threats to this nation is the Den of Thieves, liberalism, the ACLU and now a new threat, the Obama Administration. How did this man get elected, anyway" I know there are democrats out there who would vote for King Kong if he was a democrat. The same goes for liberals. They would vote for anyone liberal. There are people who just vote for change after what they have been hearing about George Bush for at least 6 years. There are always people that just want to get on the band wagon. I believe the biggest block of voters were the ones that were uninformed on who Obama really is. Every question, every doubt about him, was covered up by the *Liberal, biased press*. There are quite a few reasons why Obama is a threat to this nation. For starters, he will take this country into socialism and socialized medicine is just a start. Ask the people of France, England and Canada how bad that is for the people. Also, he, will spend us into debt to the extent that our great grandchildren will be unable to clear the debt. Now he is attacking senior health plans. I could write a whole new book on what Obama is doing to this country. I think his goal is to take all the money from the rich and give it to the poor, making us all equal, money wise.

What this Administration fails to realize is that businesses and the "rich" are needed to furnish the jobs. There have always been rich people and there have always been poor people and there always will be. The best thing *The People's Party* can do is take away some of the discomfort of the poor people.

If you really want to have a tea party, then send a message to the people in control by joining *The People's Party of America*. What chance did the people who fought against the British in The Revolutionary War think they had? (1775-1783) The Colonist only had a Militia and Loyalists. No army, no navy, but they had a principle to fight for which started as an idea to get out from under the British rule. And that, ladies and gentlemen, is exactly what we are fighting to do, get out from under a government that has gotten completely out of control. But instead of armed revolution, we are going to do it from the ballot box.

The election coming up is for seats in Congress. I say to you, "Vote out all incumbents regardless of party affiliation." To all the Democrats who are interested in our party, do not vote for another Democrat because they all stick together. You can see what has happened since the Democrats have taken over Congress. Absolutely nothing. Spend and expand government, raise taxes, it is going to get worse. I know Republicans are no better but, if enough Republicans are voted in, they can stop a lot of bad bills presented by the Democrats and Obama. It would also show the Democrats that you are fed up with their rule of Congress. At this time, they have the lowest approval rating ever and there is a reason for it.

You might have noticed that I have mentioned *The People's Party* many times in this book. I did this to get the people to thinking that this a new party and stop thinking Republican or Democrat.

It is going to be made up of the people and will be run by the people. This party is going back to what our founding fathers meant it to be. They have to get away from thinking "politics as usual."

I would like to remind the people that all the paragraphs in this book are my suggestions on what I think the Party should do when they come into power. They should adopt all that the people agree on and reject the rest. What I had in mind when making these suggestions was saving money and doing what I thought was right for the people and the country.

To the best of my knowledge and of my personal opinion and belief, everything written in this book is the truth.

I wish I was an accomplished writer and had good use of the English language but, I guess, what you see and read is what you get. I have never written a book and don't even know how to get it published. In man's world of today, I am nothing and never will be but, in God's world, I am somebody and always will be.

I am sure there will be some people out there who will say "Aren't you seeking fame and fortune by writing this book?" I tell you, if there was a way to write this book and not be known, I would do that. If there is to be any fame, which I doubt that there will be, I am not seeking it. As far as the money goes, if I do make any money, every penny will be spent getting *The People's Party* off the ground or until the Party has won a national election.

I guess I should tell the people a little about myself. I was raised in a little logging town of about 150 people (not counting the dogs), in the backwoods of Oregon, went through school there, joined the Navy, after being discharged, went through a Tech School where I took electronics, went to work for an Aerospace Company from which I retired after 32 years. I now live in Stockton, California.

In writing this book, I have gathered information from Wikipedia The True Encyclopedia, A little book called The United States Constitution by Terry L Jordan and a lot of general information taken from the Internet.

www.ingramcontent.com/pod-product-compliance
Lightning Source LLC
Chambersburg PA
CBHW021246280526
45784CB00005B/2251